"An inspired and inspiring poetry collection from an authentic, new voice. Zdravko Stefanović is a depthful explorer of the world's within."
— JEFF BROWN, author of *An Uncommon Bond* and *Soulshaping*

"*Honoring the Mystery* is a gentle and sensual invitation to explore the underworld of the ecstasy, pain, and playfulness of being. Zdravko's words seem to come from ancient places, leading you into this new kingdom of thought while shedding light on both your deepest depths and grounded humanness, effortlessly merging the two with grace. This book is mesmerizing, hypnotic, and lovely."
— VICTORIA ERICKSON, author of *Edge of Wonder* and *Rhythms and Roads*

"Zdravko Stefanović has always managed to connect to his readers on a spiritual level. His writing is beautifully poetic and has a life enhancing impact on me and my work. Whenever I am shooting on the mountains and am in trouble, something from his poetry pops up in my mind and it gives me some kind of courage to overcome the harsh climatic conditions. Honoured to have read this beautiful book before it was published."
— FAYEEM AVZL, Award-winning Filmmaker

"*Honoring the Mystery* is a captivating collection of poetry and stories, written to touch the heart of the inner lover and soul searcher within us all. Stefanović pulls you in with comforting, profound words seemingly spoken by the universe itself. As a published author myself, I found it an honor to read pages laced with not only life lessons, but a sense of magic, as well. In a world full of souls in need of hope, *Honoring the Mystery* provides just that, while simultaneously delivering a strong message of truth in self discovery. Zdravko Stefanović has a voice that needs to be heard for generations to come."

—ERIN VAN VUREN, author of *Brain Food for Big Kids,* renowned poet

"I've known Zdravko for a good few years now. I always liked him. I liked him because he is honest in his desire to push and brave in his methodology. These words of his are an honest insight into the man himself. An older soul sitting behind young eyes. A traveler with a profound respect for his roots. Here he continues to ask questions. Probing and prodding all that lives and dies around him from the physical to the spiritual world. I admire those that stay the course in their beliefs. The road is still long at such an age but all I can say is rock on brother. Rock on. Peace."

—PETER CHAFFEY, actor

Honoring the
MYSTERY

Zdravko Stefanović

ENREALMENT PRESS
TORONTO, CANADA

Published by Enrealment Press
PO Box 64
Acton, Ontario
Canada L7J 2M2

Cover photo by © Eurobanks | Shutterstock.com
Cover design by Susan Frybort. Book design by Allyson Woodrooffe (go-word.com)

Printed in the USA

Library and Archives Canada Cataloguing in Publication

Stefanovic, Zdravko, 1989-, author
    Honoring the mystery / Zdravko Stefanovic.

Poems.
Issued in print and electronic formats.
ISBN 978-0-9947843-9-1 (softcover).
ISBN 978-1-988648-00-2 (PDF)

        I. Title.

PR9145.9.S74H66 2017   821'.92   C2017-901795-0
                                       C2017-901796-9

Dedicated to the source of love and
balance inside all of us.

Dear Reader:

I have been an active, self-taught writer since 2008. I started writing because I wanted to find a method that would help me to make sense of the confusing, painful and yet beautiful aspects of this human experience. There is so much happening at one time, in this life.

My writing has taken many shapes and forms, and in the summer of 2014 it evolved into the shape and form of Poetry. It has been a beautifully liberating journey of unfolding.

In my poetry, I endeavor to hold the perspective of a gnostic observer in a dance with the ether. It is an exploratory venture into the depths of the one thing that holds everything together: Consciousness. Much like in meditation, I pay deep attention to what is going on within the realms of Soul and Psyche, and try to weave all these seemingly contradictory experiences into an alchemy of meaning.

You will hopefully,
in the play and display of syntaxed words,
experience yourself.
And this...
This is where and how we meet.

Thank you for sharing in my work.

Honoring the
MYSTERY

Zdravko Stefanović

your heart is whispering
a story that is more ancient
than the world itself.

don't hush it.
hush yourself.

listen.

#

secretly,
inside the passing
of every moment,

a new beginning,
a new love
awaits you.

welcome it.

#

Meditation,
is ultimately

the Art of listening.

Inside of you,
a Master is resting.

Awaken Him.

#

there is a broadcast by the universe
that you should
tune into.

\#

and that is why we loved
each other madly,

our love was madness,
free from human concepts.

#

she had her feet on the ground,
her heart was in peace, and her mind
in love. she was thriving.

they cursed her
for being so simple,
so ordinary.

but to him and her who had the eyes
and heart
as one;

she was a goddess in disguise,
a master of her own life,
and no insult was big
or small enough to
disturb the music
she was dancing to.

#

the key to growth
is silent reflection.

#

some people remain strangers
throughout an entire lifetime
of moments.

they just remain people,
filling a function
you can place and name like
how a certain book falls into
a specific category on the bookshelf.

but there are some,
that in one single moment
strips the disguise of being a stranger
and would never,
should never,
nor could ever

be placed in only one part of our lives.
they stream a force
that is eternally recognizeable,
but yet forever unplaceable.

cherish them,
and above all;

love them madly.

#

she had gotten tired
of being loved
like a dying flower;

picked up and left to rot.

she yearned for
someone whom she
could grow her roots with
even further and deeper than
any physical touch alone could ever
make her undergo.

she was hungry, and picky.
she craved soul,
she craved transformation.

#

what great
bravery
it must be

to act out of love,

when all other men
act like fools.

#

the heart asks
no questions.

'tis we who question
the heart.

#

jump into
the river that
aligns you with
the source of life's
greatest mysteries and
wonders.

follow that hunch.

#

the heart hurts

not when broken,
but when closed.

#

the eyes can bridge
what words can't build.

#

The same intelligence that has led
to the universe as we know it,
just so happens
to run its
course
through
you too.

When you contemplate the beauty
and wonders of this world,

understand that you, yourself,
have the exact same set of
poetic intelligence,
that in every given moment
of your life feeds you the
ability to be standing there;
contemplating it all.

#

if your love seeks affirmation,
then it is not love.

Love, is in itself,
the greatest affirmation.

#

instead of clinging
onto you;

now that i've found you,

i am, in every moment,
learning how to let you go,

only to re-discover you.

this is how my love
for you is endless.

\#

the world as she was taught it to be
was falling apart.
she stepped with her bare, dirty feet
upon the soil of her ancestors,
and in her resuming of life's
own pulse, she discovered
how beautiful it was to
rebuild something
out of pure
love.

#

an entire lifetime
spent in a day
with you,

instead of an
entire lifetime
spent in amnesia with others.

\#

fill your eyes
with the beauty
of a thousand worlds,
so that everything and everyone
you look upon feels loved.

#

the person who ever so gently
shakes the foundation of your shadowy fears,
and in your response doesn't trigger more fear,
but who's very presence instead
challenges you to

wake up
and start dreaming again,

who shows you how to love
when you are feeling most naked,

know very well then,

that you are standing face to face with love
and a soulmate of your life.

\#

i never fully told her all the details
of why and how i loved her.
some details you feel are put there
only for you to see,
only for you to preserve.

some things are simply beautiful when
they remain wild and bent by the force of
life; for a second enabling us
to get a glimpse into
the deepest and most precious
secrets of the universe.

#

she was a rankless general
in a war you couldn't win.
she wasn't a soldier nor
was she a warrior.

she was what legends were made of.

she was a hero.

#

it is when we are appreciated
fully

and looked upon with
the eyes

of loving compassion... that we dare to not retreat,
and instead choose to embrace the courageous
fire   within   our   Spirit,

so that whatever painful swamp
we have walked into,
we will;

keep unfolding,
unraveling,
learning,
marching,

to the beautiful shores of
forgiving new beginnings.

find those eyes.

look yourself in the mirror,
and love every broken, bent and polished atom
just the same.

#

when we forgive,

we love,
we heal,
we grow,
we cherish

&

we welcome every
past and future part
of our life to consume us,
in its uttermost transforming capacity.

#

we are all weaving magic into
the fabric and structure
of each others' souls.

#

He had no idea what was lying ahead of him.
He had never been thrown into a
pool of possibilities
this big.

He had never dreamed to be

dreaming this big,
this boldly,
this wisely,
this playfully.

He had never before acquired *this* vision.

All he knew was that

love is infectious;

and it had now completely taken over his system.

#

our tears contain the elixir
of our innermost beauty.

#

be like the weed that grows
in a lifeless desert.

uninterrupted by external circumstances;   .

blossom wherever,
whenever.

remain in love with life.

#

find your rhythm,
and you will find your song.

\#

Your heart is singing.
In fact, it is you, who is singing.

The song of all that is known,
The sacred landscape
is within.

Go ahead and roam.

You might simply have gotten out of balance.

Restore your rhythm,
and oh,
dear starchild,

you too;
shall sing.

#

Becoming a master of love,
essentially means becoming
a master of letting go.

Now, one shan't confuse
letting go with giving up.

To give up is to not care.
To let go is to invite freedom.

And it is when our actions are
completely free, that whatever
we touch, becomes infected with
a burning presence of timelessness.

Such love invoked is, I believe,
what untwists our hearts, or what
gives fruit its exquisite taste,
and even, if only minimalistically:

makes the Gods smile.

#

she did to me

what wisdom does to ego;

taught me how to love.

#

my only requirement
for adventure is to
have no requirements.

go nuts,

go calmly,

into the unplanned sequence
of events that thrills your soul.

#

reality is a leakage of imagination.

#

you are Art.

why settle for a draft?

#

i mean...

stars killed themselves
so that you could exist.

#

the source of
deep caring

is

unnoticable,
invisible

to the sleeping Eye.

I
(prove nothing)
and
(work diligently)

with the source.

#

we are so bound by
the mind

that when it slips,
and the heart enters,

we treat it as an
alien intruder.

such decapitation of ourselves
is what gradually
makes us unhappy.

#

without her knowing,
i had her feeling,
all the pain and loving.

without him seeing,
i felt my heart invoking,
a sense of loving understanding.

silence came,
and they felt no shame.

#

be to yourself
always accessible.

just as a flower is in full focus of

blooming,

so can you take hold
of what makes you

grow,

and bloom into beauty.

#

you show me the insides
of uncharted territories
of my own heart and imagination.

the world we live in,
have been brought up in,

taught us that time is money.

but there is no pricetag to
what you make me
see.

#

she demanded nothing.
expectations were a deathtrap.

so she dug her own path to love upon.

i slipped,
and look;

now she buried her realness into my soul.

#

take a trip through yourself.

#

Pain taught me beauty.

#

the stretchmarks of her beauty;

subtle teachers
from the past,

penetrating their wisdom
through the luster
in her eyes,
in her confusion,
in her dance.

always reminding,
in the mirror
of a lover,
a memory,
a lifetime;

she was her own master.

#

she had freedom
tattoed in her eyes.

her gaze liberated
the stories in my heart,

so that they could enter into this world,
to heal,
to transform,
and to turn this planetary adventure
into a ride

surpassing my wildest imagination.

#

your voice,

let it speak the unspeakable.

i have had enough with the loud and weak
voices
of falsehood.

#

god damn it.

you call it success,
but it is not.

it is shallowness.

the fire inside of you
is being traded for goods.

how can i ever then give you anything?

go away,

as long as my success is your failure,
we are the death of each others' souls.

#

The simplest of things can catch
our Spirit the most.
There is no need to study anything but
yourself when you are in awe,
or in love, or in confusion.

As you become truly apparent and
transparent to yourself,
nature herself,
will tell you all her secrets.

So go watch a seed sprout,
how ants cooperate,
or why silence has a substance.

#

secretly,
infuse a little love
in all that you do.

this is my secret.

#

dear child,

you must in the dusty
storms that try to
suffocate the millions
of stars inside of you,

remain strong,

and if you break into
millions of pieces;

i will help you carry
them all back to place,

and tell you the story
of how every piece of
you is destined for
great things.

#

Love is like an ocean,
whereas I am the water.

My ability to love
is only limited by
how much I dare to

truthfully express.

the truth is love.

#

examine your demons.

give them wings,
open the cage.

"begone, I am not
for you to feed upon."

#

extend,
re-define,

and

imprint the universe
with your passion,

with your Spirit.

#

when will these emotional robots
realize that they are not so much
their chips and circuits,
but the electricity
flowing inside
of them?

#

I would in her presence,
surrender to the magic
that stretched far outside of her body
and let it within me;

touch the very tissue
of that which made us both
what we were:

two mooncreatures
stuck on a paradise
far from home.

#

The restoration of trust
is a journey which we do with ourselves,
not with the other.

The road is crooked and
filled with traps,
thus only the truly brave and enduring
kind of characters venture on

the journey of forgiveness.

If all could find the strength
to go through with it,

we could, I believe, have world peace within
a generation.

#

Someone who argues that our inability to
change is due to innate, instinctive human
nature, is not presenting you
with a scientific statement.

It is someone who is either lazy
or
in love with their own comfort.

Lazyness is a disease
in thought, action, and behavior.

It is the death of change,
the death of life and
the disarming
of our Spirit.

Rid yourself from it.

#

I have felt pain.
I still do.
I know you have too.

I fear it not, for it is how
I can understand you,
truly and deeply.

Let us put quotation marks on it,
and tell it as a story to each other.

Let us elevate above the pain,
and create a presence that is
more powerful

than any bomb made by Man
and his ignorance.

Let us, dear friend,
fly together,

back to the stars
where we belong.

#

Everybody talks about
Alice in Wonderland.

What about the
Wonderland in Alice?

\#

The greatest of efforts and sacrifices
will always remain invisible to someone
who has not awoken the heart.

But you,
who have in your heart the burning flame
of the hero;

do not give way to your own impatience or the
desire of acknowledgement.

Remain humbly devoted to finding ways
of addressing the sleeping hero in
your brother's eyes.

He is there,
Slumbering in the vastness
of eternity.

#

The death of a loving life is guilt.
The death of guilt is forgiveness.

A life of forgiveness is a life of gratitude.
A life of gratitude is a happy life!

Life stops when we doubt, when we deny.

Deeply accept,
and simply move on.

#

Somewhere, in between your
screaming and dancing cells,
am I.

Melting.
At the sight of your being.

How are we so the same,
but so different?
The chaotic probabilities
of life formed us, they would say.

but oh,
my love,
fooled not be by the form!

i am inside of you,
you are inside of me.

this is love,
passing through us,
fear not the journey.

so join me,
join yourself,
let us implode together,
at the marvelous,
unexplainable magic of
human life.

\#

I wish to remind you:

a single drop of beauty
can make the entire ocean worth swimming.

this is the divine spark
that guides our footsteps
in a seemingly dark world.

the courage to speak of
hope while standing at
the edge of improbability.

it is irrational.
it is insanity and madness

but it is who and what we are.

so rejoice;

and stand above the chains of fate.

\#

in   a   part   of   me

is   the   whole   of   you.

~

a speck of dust blown away
into the vortex of the
chaotic beauty of your
temporary manifestation
and reflection of what is

eternal in me,
in you.

i surrender to every moment
of witnessing how you awake
all that is holy and sacred.

~

in   a   part   of   you

is   the   whole   of   me.

#

love her,
no need to tame her...

love will crystalize
and unite duality

into the biggest
form of knowledge.

one notion,
one aspect.

the aspect of oneness.

\#

shadow will always
accompany light.

your shadow;

instead of it leading you,
let it follow you.

\#

the warrior of love
is dancing.

you think of it
as a fight.

but it is all a dance.

#

You must remain restless in
your teaching,
your learning,
and in your
ability to love.

Bloom like a flower,
reach your fullest potential.

Remain in a constant state of growth.

#

Commitment to another person
has nothing to do with the other person.

It has to do with whether or not
we wish to allow the other to act
as the key which unlocks,
and thus;

frees the angels and demons
imprisoned
within ourselves.

#

it has come to my attention
that music,

is everything.

furthermore,
we are the conductors

of cosmic symphonies

while we,
ourselves, our lives...

are a direct result

of how we create while dancing.

#

Seldom is anything that we have been taught
anything that we truly are.

Thoughts and ideals borrowed
in exchange for our lives..

... too much of a price to pay,

so to carry the fears and burdens of lives
lived unexplored and superficially.

#

i saw it, right there in that very moment
that changes a man's life over night.

i saw in her eyes
the paradise residing
within
both of us.

where we have already re-lived
every possible way of reminding
each other

of how we all carry
the same power

used to ignite the core of newly formed
stars.

#

now that we have
found each other,

let us not
lose ourselves.

but if we do,
let our unstained love
forever be an open bridge
that helps us find our way

back to our hearts.

\#

speechlessness is the trait
of any experienced truth.

\#

Let not her body
be merely a source of pleasure.

let it be a source of healing and ecstacy.

Honor the Goddess.

#

In the richness
of your loving gaze,

I found fullness.

I found home.

#

A lot changes
when we navigate

with the universe,

instead of against it.

#

'tis the mark of a wounded Soul

to be able to see

the inside crying
of our outer smiling.

#

the heart is a pitstop
for all the darkness in the universe.

it is where it transforms into light.

#

A proper kiss can
contain all the
secrets of the universe.

\#

Love is the only contamination
worth spreading.

#

Out of order grows beauty.
Out of chaos, we grow.
Out of beauty and growth;

The ether will show,
Magic will flow,
Your circuits will glow,
Through understanding you'll row,
Your own brilliance,
Doesn't always have to make sense,
Go inside and cleanse,
Your fear and doubts,
Water your Soul's droughts,
Unite Mind with Heart,
Let down your guard,
Madness is the ultimate reward,
Wherein we turn thoughts into a diamond shard,
It ain't that hard,
The more you try the less you move forward,
Simply let go,

And unite chaos – with order.

#

I could not but love the mystery
that seemed to be what kept
that beautiful Spirit of hers
alive.

#

he belonged not to her world.

but to him,
she was his world.

and forever would he dive into
the depths of danger and peril
to find his way back to that one
and true excitement
of his Soul.

#

transformation

is the ultimate poetry

present in nature.

#

The reason why people talk
so much crap is, I believe,
due to the distance between the
brain and the mouth,
being much shorter than the distance between
the brain and the heart.

#

turn off autopilot
once in a while.

#

May forgiveness find
its way into your veins
when condemning yourself
or any other Soul,

and let it guide you to the
behavioral footsteps of love.

#

the problem with building walls
isn't only that we don't
let anyone else in.

it is that we don't
let ourselves out.

#

I find no comfort
in the ideals of
the deluded masses.

#

The greatest gift
is to give.

~

Fill yourself up,
Share the rest unconditionally,
Thus;
The less you need,
The more you can give.

Simplicity is the way
of the warrior.

He asks for nothing,
And all is to Him given.

#

There are invisible strings
stretching out from
our hearts,

waiting to establish a connection
which channels the magic
that fuels our lives.

\#

To search is futile.
To be found is the way.

#

If your love is weak,
so will all weak feed
upon thee.

If your love is strong,
so will all weak turn
into love.

#

Your task is now to be amongst
humans, animals and this spectacle
of life's endless diversity.

To bring forth a sense of
interconnectedness and unity.

To guide yourself
and others,
to the shimmering
chambers of memory,
where the tissue of love can
be woven into all that you do,
and create a story that will clear
any confusion and worry in their hearts
as to where we all belong.

We belong right here, together, in unison
with the miracle and spectacle we call
life.

#

They said time would change
me and everything around me.

Now, I understand,
it is love,
that changes everything;

even time itself,
crumbles
in the hands of love.

#

Goddess is a description of radiance,
not of appearance.

#

My point is perhaps
not your point.

This is however,
not my point.

I love you regardless,
that is my point.

#

Don't play me like
one of your pawns in
a game you've already mastered.

Play me like a violin,

in an act of

unrepeatable symphony

of loving madness.

Let us destroy and rebuild
each other with the
authenticity of
our Spirits.

Show me a song I have not
heard before.

Show me what music I never thought
my life could play.

#

When all your pain collides,
beware of not retreating;

for this is the breaking point.

Once we have broken the confines of
all that has held us back;

there can only be progress,
growth,
healing.

A rapid state of evolution,
followed by an immense
state of ecstacy.

#

First,
Awaken to your own magic.

Then wake it up in others.

#

Be able to hear when
someone is opening
themselves up to you.

Some of them
have been under the ground
for a long time.

Your reaction can either
help them sprout, or bury
them back even deeper.

#

your consciousness will expand
as you align yourself
closer to its
source.

#

Love is a seed

that grows

upon itself.

And we,
well,
we are its soil.

\#

shallow beauty,
shallow understanding.

#

My life is a dream within a dream,
and I am not the dreamer.

I am the witness of this human extension
of the creative force that creates
these dreams.

#

It is utterly hard to grasp unless
granted access to the
backstage machinery of sensory input and
beyond
the limitations of humanly designed
software
of mind and psyche,

but within the psychedelic
or transcendental realm
one can see how

the universe grows through us.

what we have simply worded to be thoughts,
emotions, memories and dreams,

are all but different channels
of input where the universe
through us;

grows.

and in the process of doing so,
it tells us the story of our lives.

#

fear not of breaking.

I promise you,
all your pieces
will be painfully
but yet gently
polished and
improved by the same force
that formed our paradise of a planet out of
scattered debris roaming lonely across the
vastness of space.

with enough gravity,
with enough love,
time will end,
and so will
your pain.

#

"i can't explain it"
she said.

"you don't have to.

I feel that our love stems from
a place far away from here.

Perhaps it is our future selves
sending that which we call love,
back to our past selves...

... so to try and make sure
that *nothing*
makes us believe we won't
be together forever.

to avoid our own oblivion,
we have figured out the
language of eternity,

and it might just be love."

#

the dream
is not a dream.

it is a gateway,
a portal,
a door,

into the halls
of eternity.

#

that's what it's all about:

making time envious
because we managed
to stop it.

#

*in*tuition.

to be *in tune* with
the universe.

'ts the radio station
of Spirit.

#

What made her beautiful,
and I mean really beautiful,
the kind of beauty that shines
and dazzles you to leave you blind;

is that she knew that she
housed the universe
inside of her.

it was in her every move.

she was infested with knowledge

and it made me love her beyond
the point of madness.

#

Your heart cannot break
if it's already open.

#

Love is what I teach.

Love is how I learn.

#

Link not only your bodies.
Link your minds,
Link your breathing.

Synchronize completely;
Two beings into one.

#

It's the experience of great
beauty that brings me to
the center of Spirit.

\#

and all of a sudden
you know,
this awakening hits you.

you just sort of open your eyes
as if for the first time

and all the noise in the world

turns into music.

you lean your head back
look at the sky

and wonder;

why have I never seen the beauty in blue?

\#

it is in love,
and only in love
that we can transcend.

our thinking,
our behavior,
our limitations.

Peel slowly child,
the outer layers
of your coal-covered
surface.

See that you are a
diamond shining
just as bright
as the stars of the night sky.

#

You cannot think love.

Just love.

#

Just look up,
and know;

we gaze upon the same stars.

That alone,
can abolish

all sense of separation.

#

We kept finding love

where only the brave
ventured freely.

in the joy of
madness.

\#

make love in the sunset

enter a new country
completely stoned

share a 100-year-old
whiskey with a stranger.

sometimes,

disassemble whatever
borderline-acceptable
notions have been put
in your head by those
who worshipped comfort

including those put there by yourself.

#

Randomness is just Man's
way of saying that he does
not yet fully understand.

\#

The ocean within

can either make me drown

or turn me into a sailor

that in his screams

thanks the winds of currents
for the ability to be dancing
with the waves.

#

Hold me forever, she said.

This, I cannot do, I said.

But in me,
and in you,

the forever
lives inside of us.

This, I will help you remember.

#

A proper redirection of your attention
can bring beautiful things
into your life.

#

Change the world,
brick by brick.

show unexpected
love and kindness.

This will,
I strongly believe;

re-write patterns in our brain
responsible for autonomous behavior.

the eradication of
negative stereotyping.

\#

I am a warrior of the
noble Art;

I protect and help establish
the kind of value
that awakens
the Soul.

#

Sprinkle some
of your magic

wherever you go.

\#

The mask you are wearing
is wearing you down.

\#

Making the chaos simple
is the master's initiation
to his own Art.

#

Presence is the soil of all our actions.

If we are present, we are able
to see deeply into any situation.

It is in the depth of presence where all
things
grow and die.

It is where *essence* remains unformed,
and where we find any type of power.

#

She was filled with substance
that only a few could
ever touch or
awaken.

We were both
entranced with
her magic.

\#

We all rise and fall.

The trick is to welcome
and be able to enjoy both,
equally as much.

Instead of seeking refuge
in the few trees we've
managed to climb,

we should master the art
of climbing, so that we
can climb all trees.

In doing so,
we can love the entire forest,
and all of its wilderness.

#

Master your storm,
(and you will)
master yourself.

#

Let your own magic
be everything
you need.

#

Sometimes,

be completely still.

Let this world
reflect the beauty
you possess.

#

I am fairly convinced that

birdsongs are in fact

birds laughing.

a symphony of joy.

#

the top of the food chain
fails to describe that which
can devour us without having
to tear our bodies into shreds.

instead of calling it the food chain,
call it the chain of energy.

oh,

beware of Humans when they are turning
into a toothless predator.

Their bite is not from this world.

#

she haunts me in my dreams.

like a butterfly,

her patterned wings scared
only those who had never seen
her fly.

but i had seen her fly,
with me.

not only in our dreams,
but somewhere far away,
we had given each other wings.

now only my dreams seem able
to cope with what life never
seemed to be able to sustain;

the love of two caterpillars.

\#

Earth was to be our Mothership,
and we Her captains.

then we just started
watching TV instead.

\#

all she wanted was to be allowed
to dance with the fairies.

to let herself be captivated by
their vivid stories of a world
where kings and queens fought
noone else but those who had in their
souls a burning hatred to extinguish
the fiery melodies
of the music that made the entire world spin.

(she passionately explained that)

the fairies told stories

where the true rulers
were those who ruled in
coherence with their
dancing people.

an entire kingdom
dancing.

#

dear starchild,
you who embody the universe.

take a deep look
into your own beauty.

i will,
if you get lost in
the shadowy darkness,

help you

notice the glowing star

of your own being.

#

I fought demons my
entire life,

not knowing it was a
neverending battle.

the more we fought,
the more I became like them.

Then,
one day,

I aligned with the source,
and we all found
our way home.

#

Beauty, has ultimately
nothing to do with the body.

It has however, everything
to do with how the immortal Soul
embodies a mortal body as a method
of expressing immortality on a mortal
plane.

That design, that paradox,
is in itself,

worth the contemplation of a thousand
lifetimes.

#

The key to Spirit,
love and magic,
is not found
in things,
places
or in
pleasures.

It is found in the depth of presence.

#

I roam in the center of all things.

It is there that the Soul of Man
finds its restful teachings.

#

A society that
has lost the
ability to
establish
value
is doomed
to drown in
ignorance.

#

tame your own madness
and yet,
remain wild.

this, is the trick.

#

The future is not something
far away, that is to be
carefully planned.

It is here, right now,
merging with you.

The future is imminent.

#

The passing of moments
is eternal.

Passing we naturally understand.

Inside of welcoming
the next moment,
we have the learning,

and
where the mystery reveals itself.

#

touch the source.

fall madly in love
with existence,

with yourself.

#

About the Author

A very popular social media poet, Zdravko Stefanović has devoted much of his life to exploring the mysteries that lie within us. Growing up in Sweden, he spent considerable time in nature, honing his perceptions and connecting with a deeper understanding of our universal experience. Nature became an embracive force to reckon with, to befriend, to understand, and to communicate with. As a result, his writing has an uncanny ability to touch the timely and the timeless, inviting the reader to connect deeply with the moment, while simultaneously contemplating questions of deeper meaning. Honoring the Mystery is his first published collection.

\#